LEADER'S GUIDE

WIN
with
PEOPLE

Returning TO THE
Call OF A *Shepherd*

Win with People Leader's Guide

www.leadtowin.com
ISBN: 978-1-954961-23-4

Printed in the United States.

CONTENTS

IF YOU'RE READY TO LEAD AN INSPIRED TEAM,

THEN THIS GUIDE IS FOR YOU.

I'm honored that you're investing in your leadership and in the people God has entrusted to you. I don't take that lightly. You and I both know that ministry isn't just about filling seats or running programs—it's about shepherding real people with real struggles toward the life-changing power of Jesus.

That's why I wrote *Win with People*—not as a leadership theory, but as a call to action, a call back to the heart of the shepherd.

> **This guide is designed to be a complement to the book—practical, actionable, and immediately impactful for your team.**

> **The work you do with your team today will produce shepherds who will go on to raise even more shepherds.**

The mission hasn't changed. Jesus said, "Feed My sheep." That's what we do. And the best way to expand our reach is by pouring into the people already at our side. Let's develop leaders who love, lead, and multiply.

Cheering you on,
Jeff Little

HOW THIS GUIDE WORKS

Rally Your Team

1. **Invite your team to participate.**

Teams/groups that will benefit from this journey:

- Senior Leadership Team/Department Heads/Campus Team
- Student Ministry Team
- Kids Ministry Team
- Ministries/Departments (Ex. Worship, Production, Connections, Business Office)
- High-Capacity Volunteers/Core Leaders

2. **Get a copy of the book *Win with People* for each person.**

3. **Schedule meetings with your team.**

You can add this time to your regularly scheduled department/team meetings or choose a dedicated time to meet and talk through the book.

Here are two scheduling options:

- Meet for 6 weeks, and plan to discuss two chapters in *Win with People* (and the corresponding sessions in this guide) per week.

- Meet for 12 weeks, and plan to discuss one chapter/session per week.

Before Meeting with Your Team

- Read the corresponding chapter in the *Win with People* book.

- Skim the session content from this guide that your team will be working through.

- Prep your thoughts on the “Talk About It” sections.

During the Discussions

- When it comes to being open and honest, go first.

- Create space for real conversations.

- Lead with the belief that God has great things in store for your team on the backside of this experience.

Note: The 6-week and 12-week meeting schedules are only suggestions. Plan to stay flexible—if a certain session/chapter is resonating with your team, or you need more time, feel free to take multiple meetings to discuss before you move on to the next session.

SESSION

1

WHY DO WE NEED TO WIN WITH PEOPLE?

A great church is built on a group of people who are committed to God's vision, who are willing to sacrifice for that vision, and who are consistently inviting others to become a part of that vision.

—

Win with People, p. 11

SESSION PREP

Before you meet with your team to work through this session:

- ☐ **Book** | Read the introduction and chapter 1 in *Win with People*. Highlight anything that grabs your attention.

- ☐ **Leader Guide** | Skim the chapter 1 discussion questions and application steps on pages 11-12. (They also appear in the book at the end of chapter 1.) Note the ones that are most relevant to your team right now.

- ☐ **Leader Guide** | Preview the "Talk About It" section so you can lead the discussion with thoughtful input.

SESSION GOAL

Keep these two things in mind:

- The point of chapter 1 in *Win with People*, "Why Do We Need to Win with People?," is that the call to ministry is to love and serve people on behalf of Jesus. He said that if we love Him, we'll feed His sheep.

- The goal of this session is to inspire your team to pursue their purpose with passion, which is to reflect the intention, compassion, and sacrifice of our Good Shepherd, Jesus.

Talk About It

Since you may not have time to address everything in this section, note the questions that are most relevant to your team and start with those.

1. The questions in the following box appear at the end of chapter 1 in *Win with People*. Ask your team to share a few of their responses.

DISCUSSION

1. How does the simplicity of "Feed. My. Sheep." shape your understanding of ministry? What would it look like in your role to "Feed. My. Sheep."?
2. How have you seen comparison negatively impact a ministry or team? Could this have been avoided? How?
3. Describe where you see yourself in relation to your ministry calling.

APPLICATION

1. **Personal Reflection:** Spend 10 minutes reflecting on your call to ministry.
2. How did you receive that call from Jesus, and how did you feel when you first said "Yes"?

   A. What did you think your "Yes" would entail?

   B. How does reflecting on your initial calling impact your current perspective of ministry?

3. **Action Step:** Think of a church staff member or volunteer you can encourage this week.

   A. What's a contribution they have made recently that you can affirm?

   B. Write them a note, send a message, or thank them in person for what they do.

2. Read Ephesians 4:11-13 below. Then, ask your team to engage with the following questions, being mindful that the second one will take real courage to answer:

EPHESIANS 4:11-13

So Christ himself gave the apostles, the prophets, the evangelists, the pastors and teachers, to equip his people for works of service, so that the body of Christ may be built up until we all reach unity in the faith and in the knowledge of the Son of God and become mature, attaining to the whole measure of the fullness of Christ.

- Why did God design ministry as a team effort?

- What kind of teammate are you? Are you known by those you work with as an encourager or reserved in your praise? Are you known as someone who focuses more on your individual role or on serving the needs of the team? Are you known for being proactive or reactive?

3. Copy the following grid on a whiteboard. Then, ask your team to fill in the grid.

Team Member	A Primary Strength	How This Strength Best Serves the Team

Win This Week

Give the following challenge to your team, and then close in prayer.

In the next several days, find one moment where you feel the urge to react toward someone else—whether in frustration, defensiveness, or withdrawal—and pause to practice the shepherding mindset by extending compassion instead.

Come to the next meeting ready to share how this interaction went.

Note: At the end of each session, you'll find a "Win This Week" challenge like this one to give to your team. These challenges have been customized to this guide. But if you'd rather choose an Action Step from the end of each chapter in Win with People, that content is printed in this guide for your convenience.

SESSION

2

SHEPHERDS SMELL LIKE SHEEP

Shepherds want more *FOR*
the sheep than they want *FROM* them.

Win with People, p. 20

SESSION PREP

Before you meet with your team to work through this session:

- ☐ **Book** | Read chapter 2 in *Win with People*. Highlight anything that grabs your attention.
- ☐ **Leader Guide** | Skim the chapter 2 discussion questions and application steps on page 18. (They also appear in the book at the end of chapter 2.) Note the ones that are most relevant to your team right now.
- ☐ **Leader Guide** | Preview the "Talk About It" section so you can lead the discussion with thoughtful input.

SESSION GOAL

Keep these two things in mind:

- The point of chapter 2 in *Win with People*, "Shepherds Smell Like Sheep," is that ministry is about embracing the challenging-but-rewarding work of caring for God's people—His sheep. And you can only take care of the sheep if you're close to them. Shepherding is not a remote job.
- The goal of this session is to help your team see their primary job in ministry as being shepherds of God's flock.

Follow-Up, Session 1

Circle back to the "Win This Week" challenge given at the end of session 1 by asking your team the questions below.

In session 1, you were challenged to practice the shepherding mindset by extending compassion when tempted to react in frustration, defensiveness, or withdrawal.

- What type of situation provoked your initial reaction?
- How easy or difficult was it to respond differently in the moment?

Talk About It

Since you may not have time to address everything in this section, note the questions that are most relevant to your team and start with those.

1. The questions in the following box appear at the end of chapter 2 in *Win with People*. Ask your team to share a few of their responses.

DISCUSSION

1. "If you're called to ministry, people ARE the job." How does this statement affect your role in ministry, regardless of what that role might be?

2. What should the goal of the shepherd/pastor be? How is this goal counter-cultural?

3. What are some of the misplaced goals we sometimes have in ministry?

APPLICATION

1. **Personal Reflection:** Spend time evaluating your current role in ministry.

   A. Have you fully embraced the fact that "people ARE the job," or have you lost sight of that focus?

   B. How can you make what you do more about the people you serve?

2. **Action Step:** Think of one or two people in your church whom you can serve this week.

   A. Write down their names.

   B. What do they need from you? How can you add value to their lives?

   C. Commit to serving them this week.

2. Read 1 Peter 5:2-4 below. Then, have your team engage with the following questions.

1 PETER 5:2-4

Be shepherds of God's flock that is under your care, watching over them—not because you must, but because you are willing, as God wants you to be; not pursuing dishonest gain, but eager to serve; not lording it over those entrusted to you, but being examples to the flock. And when the Chief Shepherd appears, you will receive the crown of glory that will never fade away.

- This passage calls us to shepherd ***willingly*** and ***eagerly***, not for personal gain. How does this challenge the way you're currently approaching ministry?

- What circumstances would you point to that are keeping you from shepherding willingly and eagerly?

3. Shepherding is not a remote job. What are some specific situations you learned about recently only because you were spending time with people in your church?

Note your team's input on a whiteboard version of this grid:

People We Talked With	Challenges They're Facing

Before moving on, see how the team might answer these questions:

- How satisfied are you with how quickly these interactions came to mind for our team?
- What do our answers reveal about our current priorities?
- What could we do as a team to elevate the goal of "smelling like sheep"?

Win This Week

Give the following challenge to your team, and then close in prayer.

Spend time with someone in your church outside of your normal ministry responsibilities. Consider a casual coffee meeting, a simple text exchange, or a phone call to check in and ask how you can be praying for them.

Come to the next meeting ready to share how the touchpoint encouraged you in your role.

SESSION

3

GOD'S HEART FOR PEOPLE (HIS SHEEP)

If we're going to fulfill God's call for our life,
we need to have God's heart for people.

—

Win with People, p. 35

SESSION PREP

Before you meet with your team to work through this session:

- ☐ **Book** | Read chapter 3 in *Win with People*. Highlight anything that grabs your attention.

- ☐ **Leader Guide** | Skim the chapter 3 discussion questions and application steps on page 26. (They also appear in the book at the end of chapter 3.) Note the ones that are most relevant to your team right now.

- ☐ **Leader Guide** | Preview the "Talk About It" section so you can lead the discussion with thoughtful input.

SESSION GOAL

Keep these two things in mind:

- The point of chapter 3 in *Win with People*, "God's Heart for People (His Sheep)," is that because we have the Spirit of God living inside of us, we can see people the way He sees them, care for them the way He cares for them, and love them the way He loves them.

- The goal of this session is to inspire your team to model the security, power, and grace of our Good Shepherd so that the sheep they're serving will someday long to do the same.

Follow-Up, Session 2

Circle back to the "Win This Week" challenge given at the end of session 2 by asking your team the questions below.

In session 2, you were given the challenge of spending time with someone outside of your normal ministry responsibilities.

- How did it go?
- What insights did you gain?

Talk About It

Since you may not have time to address everything in this section, note the questions that are most relevant to your team and start with those.

1. The questions in the following box appear at the end of chapter 3 in *Win with People*. Ask your team to share a few of their responses.

DISCUSSION

1. Do you have God's heart for people? How can you grow in this area?

2. What makes someone feel "seen"? Do you think the people you pastor, lead, or work with feel seen by you?

3. Do you see yourself as a sheep? Why is this important?

APPLICATION

1. **Personal Reflection:** Read Psalm 23 again.

    A. How does this psalm speak to you today?

    B. What needs or concerns are you carrying that this psalm addresses?

    C. Why is it important to apply Psalm 23 to yourself before leading others?

2. **Action Step:** Look at the sheep characteristics on page 38 again.

    A. Write down a few characteristics that stand out to you.

    B. What is something you can do this week to apply these to the people you serve?

2. Read Matthew 9:35-36 below. Then, ask your team the following two questions.

MATTHEW 9:35-36

Jesus went through all the towns and villages, teaching in their synagogues, proclaiming the good news of the kingdom and healing every disease and sickness. When he saw the crowds, he had compassion on them, because they were harassed and helpless, like sheep without a shepherd.

- What do you see when you look out at the people in our church?

- What are the current obstacles that keep us from seeing people the way Jesus does?

3. Have your team look up Ezekiel 34:11-16, which is printed for you on the following page. Talk about the three questions that follow, noting your team's input on a whiteboard.

EZEKIEL 34:11-16

"'For this is what the Sovereign Lord says: I myself will search for my sheep and look after them. As a shepherd looks after his scattered flock when he is with them, so will I look after my sheep. I will rescue them from all the places where they were scattered on a day of clouds and darkness. I will bring them out from the nations and gather them from the countries, and I will bring them into their own land. I will pasture them on the mountains of Israel, in the ravines and in all the settlements in the land. I will tend them in a good pasture, and the mountain heights of Israel will be their grazing land. There they will lie down in good grazing land, and there they will feed in a rich pasture on the mountains of Israel. I myself will tend my sheep and have them lie down, declares the Sovereign Lord. I will search for the lost and bring back the strays. I will bind up the injured and strengthen the weak, but the sleek and the strong I will destroy. I will shepherd the flock with justice.'"

- How does God describe His role as a shepherd?

- What are practical ways that we can reflect this kind of care in our leadership?

- What divine resources does God offer to us that might help us?

Win This Week

Give the following challenge to your team, and then close in prayer.

In a conversation you have this week, try being mindful of how you're engaging in it. Instead of cutting off the other person, interrupting, or jumping in to relate to what they're saying by sharing your own experience, focus on asking meaningful follow-up questions like:

- "What motivated you to respond that way?"
- "How did that make you feel?"
- "How did your actual experience compare with your expectations?"
- "What has this experience taught you?"
- "What's been the (hardest/best/most gratifying) part for you?"
- "How can I support or pray for you in this?"
- "Looking back, what do you think God might be showing you through this?"

Come to the next meeting ready to share how the experience impacted you.

SESSION

4

JESUS, THE CHIEF SHEPHERD

If we want to return to the call of being a shepherd, we have to know how the Chief Shepherd does it.

Win with People, p. 53

SESSION PREP

Before you meet with your team to work through this session:

- ☐ **Book** | Read chapter 4 in *Win with People*. Highlight anything that grabs your attention.

- ☐ **Leader Guide** | Skim the chapter 4 discussion questions and application steps on page 34. (They also appear in the book at the end of chapter 4.) Note the ones that are most relevant to your team right now.

- ☐ **Leader Guide** | Preview the "Talk About It" section so you can lead the discussion with thoughtful input.

SESSION GOAL

Keep these two things in mind:

- The point of chapter 4 in *Win with People*, "Jesus, the Chief Shepherd," is two-fold: First, we have a Good Shepherd in Jesus, who calls us, not because He needs us but because He wants to include us. Second, we become more effective in our role as shepherds of God's flock as we learn to serve like Jesus.

- The goal of this session is to remind your team that the ultimate goal in this "shepherding approach" to ministry is to stay as close as possible to Jesus daily.

Follow-Up, Session 3

Circle back to the "Win This Week" challenge given at the end of session 3 by asking your team the questions below.

In session 3, you were given the challenge of engaging in a conversation by asking thoughtful follow-up questions.

- Who was your conversation with?
- How did it go?

Talk About It

Since you may not have time to address everything in this section, note the questions that are most relevant to your team and start with those.

1. The questions in the following box appear at the end of chapter 4 in *Win with People*. Ask your team to share a few of their responses.

DISCUSSION

1. "The greatest catalyst for change will always be our relationship with Jesus." How would you describe your relationship with Jesus right now?

2. What stands out to you from this chapter about the Chief Shepherd and what He does for the sheep?

3. As an undershepherd, how well are you following the example of the Chief Shepherd?

APPLICATION

1. **Personal Reflection:** How long has it been since you spent meaningful time with the Chief Shepherd?

   A. Are you allowing Him to minister to you and to meet your needs?

   B. Spend time seeking Him. Use the space below to write down anything you sense Him saying.

2. **Action Step:** Is there someone you know who is "lost" right now?

   A. Who is it?

   B. What does God want you to do to help reach this person?

2. Ask your team to consider the following questions regarding maintaining a close connection to Jesus:

    - What does it mean for you to be "closely connected to Jesus"?

    - What's true in your life and leadership when you're closely connected to Him?

    - How can we as a team be closely connected to Jesus?

3. Read John 10:12-13 below. Then, have your team engage with the questions that follow.

JOHN 10:12-13

"The hired hand is not the shepherd and does not own the sheep. So when he sees the wolf coming, he abandons the sheep and runs away. Then the wolf attacks the flock and scatters it. The man runs away because he is a hired hand and cares nothing for the sheep."

- Consider writing down the following grid on a whiteboard to include your team's input as you work through it. Think of scenarios that work best in your context.

The Scenario	How a Shepherd Might Respond	How a Hired Hand Might Respond
Ex. A leadership decision causes conflict among a volunteer team.	• Listens to various perspectives • Works toward consensus • Focuses on unity	• Reinforces position • Harshly requires compliance • Doesn't seek consensus

- What are some shepherding characteristics we want to commit to model as a team for this specific ministry season to ensure that "hired-hand" attitudes and actions don't sneak in? (Ex. We walk in unity with our teammates; we're humble servants; we're marked by integrity and faithfulness.)

Win This Week

Give the following challenge to your team, and then close in prayer.

Before the next meeting, find a way to put into practice one of the team commitments we made. (Ex. We walk in unity with our teammates.)

Come ready to share how things went.

SESSION

5

THE CALL TO THE SHEPHERD'S LIFE

The role of the pastor (shepherd) is not to do all the ministry. It's to equip the people to do ministry.

—

Win with People, p. 72

SESSION PREP

Before you meet with your team to work through this session:

- ☐ **Book** | Read chapter 5 in *Win with People*. Highlight anything that grabs your attention.

- ☐ **Leader Guide** | Skim the chapter 5 discussion questions and application steps on page 40. (They also appear in the book at the end of chapter 5.) Note the ones that are most relevant to your team right now.

- ☐ **Leader Guide** | Preview the "Talk About It" section so you can lead the discussion with thoughtful input.

SESSION GOAL

Keep these two things in mind:

- ▶ The point of chapter 5 in *Win with People*, "The Call to the Shepherd's Life," is that vocational ministry is a God-given calling that tests our hearts and our motivation in life. If we are called, we love our calling. We pursue it faithfully. And we gravitate toward service in a local church.

- ▶ The goal of this session is to help your team understand and better steward their calling to vocational ministry.

Follow-Up, Session 4

Circle back to the "Win This Week" challenge given at the end of session 4 by asking your team the questions below.

In session 4, you were given the challenge of putting into practice one of our team commitments.

- What situation prompted the opportunity?
- Share how it went.

Talk About It

Since you may not have time to address everything in this section, note the questions that are most relevant to your team and start with those.

1. The questions in the following box appear at the end of chapter 5 in *Win with People*. Ask your team to share a few of their responses.

DISCUSSION

1. How would you describe the difference between a career and a calling? Do we sometimes (mistakenly) blend the two? Explain.

2. "The role of the pastor (shepherd) is not to do all the ministry. It's to equip the people to do ministry." How does this statement change your perspective on ministry?

3. Look back at the seven characteristics related to calling in this chapter. Which of these characteristics speaks to you or challenges you the most right now?

APPLICATION

1. **Personal Reflection:** How well do you balance doing ministry with equipping others to do the work?

    A. What's something you are doing well to equip others?

    B. How do you need to grow in this area?

2. **Action Step:** Choose one of the following actions to implement this week:

    A. Identify a ministry task you can delegate to others.

    B. Identify someone you can mentor or train to take on a specific ministry role.

    C. Invite someone to shadow you during a specific task, then debrief with them on what they learned.

2. Revisit Ephesians 4:11-13, from session 1, which is printed below. Then, have your team answer the questions that follow.

EPHESIANS 4:11-13

So Christ himself gave the apostles, the prophets, the evangelists, the pastors and teachers, to equip his people for works of service, so that the body of Christ may be built up until we all reach unity in the faith and in the knowledge of the Son of God and become mature, attaining to the whole measure of the fullness of Christ.

- When you think of your current role, do you tend to focus more on your direct responsibilities and obligations or on how you'll equip others to get plugged into ministry?

- What does Ephesians 4:11-13 say is the reason for equipping others for works of service?

- What do you think this passage is implying about what happens when those of us in vocational ministry *don't* equip God's people for works of service?

- What would change in your daily work if you elevated the goal of equipping others for service?

Win This Week

Give the following challenge to your team, and then close in prayer.

Make a list of a few potential/future ministry leaders you could help equip. These may be people currently serving in your ministry area, people you have heard about from others, or students/kids who are growing in their gifts.

Come back to the next meeting ready to discuss who you have on your list and what steps you could give them to help them grow.

SESSION 6

PRACTICAL WAYS YOUR CHURCH CAN WIN WITH PEOPLE

The foundation for being a shepherd is
to be aware of your own wants and needs,
and to set them aside to care for the sheep.

—

Win with People, p. 87

SESSION PREP

Before you meet with your team to work through this session:

- ☐ **Book** | Read chapter 6 in *Win with People.* Highlight anything that grabs your attention.

- ☐ **Leader Guide** | Skim the chapter 6 discussion questions and application steps on page 46. (They also appear in the book at the end of chapter 6.) Note the ones that are most relevant to your team right now.

- ☐ **Leader Guide** | Preview the "Talk About It" section so you can lead the discussion with thoughtful input.

SESSION GOAL

Keep these two things in mind:

- The point of chapter 6 in *Win with People*, "Practical Ways Your Church Can Win with People," is that our churches have distinctive cultures that people can feel when they first walk in. And regardless of what else defines our culture, we must remember our highest priority is to create opportunities where people can easily encounter God.

- The goal of this session is to compel your team to rethink how guests may feel at your church and to take action to close any gaps.

Follow-Up, Session 5

Circle back to the "Win This Week" challenge given at the end of session 5 by asking your team the questions below.

In session 5, you were challenged to identify a few future/potential ministry leaders you could help equip.

- Who is on your list?
- What are a few steps you could take with them to help them grow?

Note: As the team leader, address any concerns you may have regarding what your team has shared here and have individual conversations if necessary to set clear expectations or redirect.

Talk About It

Since you may not have time to address everything in this section, note the questions that are most relevant to your team and start with those.

1. The questions in the following box appear at the end of chapter 6 in *Win with People*. Ask your team to share a few of their responses.

DISCUSSION

1. Honestly assess the question: *How would I feel if I came to my church for the first time?*

2. "The foundation for being a shepherd is to be aware of your own wants and needs, and to set them aside to care for the sheep." What does this mean?

3. What are some practical ways you can help guests at your church feel welcomed, valued, and loved?

APPLICATION

1. **Personal Reflection:** After reading this chapter, what practical takeaways can you apply to your church to create a more welcoming environment?

2. **Action Step:**

   A. What is one specific action step you can take this week to make your church more welcoming to first-time guests?

   B. How can you personally contribute to this action step?

2. Consider taking a walk through your church's main entrance and common areas as a team. Guide your team through an assessment of your church's culture by asking the following questions:

- What was your experience like the first time you came to our church?

- What's working and what's not working in our main gathering areas? Are signs clear? Is it easy to park? Do our spaces seem well maintained?

- How does our physical space make people feel? Warm and invited? Overwhelmed and anxious? Something else?

- What do our people and practices reveal to guests about who we are and who God is?

- What are we doing well? What could we do better?

3. As members of our team, when was the last time we paid careful attention to the same resources that visitors to our church might see prior to (or upon) setting foot on our property? (Offer up some of the options below to your team.)

    - ☐ Church website
    - ☐ Social media
    - ☐ Videos of worship services
    - ☐ Billboards, ads, etc.
    - ☐ Mailers/Yard signs
    - ☐ Google results on our church
    - ☐ Our parking lot
    - ☐ Our kids' check-in process
    - ☐ Our kids'/students' services
    - ☐ Our worship center sound
    - ☐ Our worship center lighting
    - ☐ Our worship center seating
    - ☐ Our guest reception area
    - ☐ Something else

Win This Week

Give the following challenge to your team, and then close in prayer.

As you come to church this weekend, think about what it might feel like to be a first-time guest. Afterwards, pick one thing you'd do to make our church environment more welcoming. Think of some ways you can be part of the solution.

Come to the next meeting ready to share.

SESSION

7

THE SHEPHERD'S MOST IMPORTANT CHALLENGE

We're the most difficult person to lead because we are all victims to our own blind spots.

—

Win with People, p. 110

SESSION PREP

Before you meet with your team to work through this session:

- ☐ **Book** | Read chapter 7 in *Win with People*. Highlight anything that grabs your attention.

- ☐ **Leader Guide** | Skim the chapter 7 discussion questions and application steps on page 52. (They also appear in the book at the end of chapter 7.) Note the ones that are most relevant to your team right now.

- ☐ **Leader Guide** | Preview the "Talk About It" section so you can lead the discussion with thoughtful input.

SESSION GOAL

Keep these two things in mind:

- ▶ The point of chapter 7 in *Win with People*, "The Shepherd's Most Important Challenge," is that despite all the challenges that spiritual shepherds face, the most important challenge is learning how to lead oneself.

- ▶ The goal of this session is to inspire your team to regularly assess themselves based on their character, competency, and curiosity.

Follow-Up, Session 6

Circle back to the "Win This Week" challenge given at the end of session 6 by asking your team the questions below.

In session 6, you were given the challenge of coming to church with the mindset of a first-time guest and evaluating how welcoming the environment feels.

- What observations did you make?
- What would you like to see improved?
- How can you help be a part of the solution?

Talk About It

Since you may not have time to address everything in this section, note the questions that are most relevant to your team and start with those.

1. The questions in the following box appear at the end of chapter 7 in *Win with People*. Ask your team to share a few of their responses.

DISCUSSION

1. "The shepherd's most important challenge is learning to lead themselves." Do you agree with that assessment? Explain.

2. Why is pride so dangerous, especially for those in ministry?

3. Who have you given permission to correct and coach you? Why is this important?

APPLICATION

1. **Personal Reflection:** Spend time reflecting on the areas of character, competency, and curiosity presented in this chapter.

    A. How are you doing in each area?

    B. Are there any changes you need to make?

2. **Action Step:** Select one of the 3 Cs (character, competency, and curiosity) to focus on for the next 30 days:

    A. Choose a goal for that area.

    B. Commit to taking intentional steps toward that goal every day for the next month.

2. How do you feel about the idea that you are the most challenging person you will ever lead?

3. Of the reasons noted in this week's chapter for why self-leadership is so difficult, which resonates with you the most?

    - ☐ **We have blind spots.** | This might show up in a lack of self-awareness, the propensity to deal with the same problems repeatedly without growing from them, or unintentionally being insensitive in conversation with others.
    - ☐ **We have prideful spirits.** | This might show up in an abrasive communication style, an unteachable spirit, or the tendency to think one knows it all.
    - ☐ **We have selfish motivations.** | This might show up in someone prioritizing their own comfort or success over others' needs, engaging with people because of what they can get instead of what they can give, and taking credit but deflecting responsibility.
    - ☐ **Something else?**

4. One of the primary ways that we can overcome the challenges of self-leadership is by growing and developing spiritually, personally, and professionally. What does your development strategy include? How did you arrive at that strategy? How is it working for you?

Win This Week

Give the following challenge to your team, and then close in prayer.

Choose one of the 3 Cs (Character, Competency, or Curiosity) and commit to focusing on it for the next seven days. Below is an idea for each:

1. **Character** | Identify a specific area in your life where you could be more honest or humble. Take intentional steps this week to address it.

2. **Competency** | Choose a new skill or area of knowledge that will help you better serve your church or team. Dedicate time each week to learning something new.

3. **Curiosity** | Commit to seeking feedback from a trusted mentor, team member, or peer. Ask them where they see room for growth in you and what advice they would offer for your leadership journey. Come to the next meeting ready to share how the touchpoint encouraged you in your role.

SESSION

8

WIN WITH YOUR TEAM

Ministry is a team sport—
the best flocks are led by teams of shepherds.

—

Win with People, p. 125

SESSION PREP

Before you meet with your team to work through this session:

- ☐ **Book** | Read chapter 8 in *Win with People*. Highlight anything that grabs your attention.

- ☐ **Leader Guide** | Skim the chapter 8 discussion questions and application steps on pages 58-59. (They also appear in the book at the end of chapter 8.) Note the ones that are most relevant to your team right now.

- ☐ **Leader Guide** | Preview the "Talk About It" section so you can lead the discussion with thoughtful input.

SESSION GOAL

Keep these two things in mind:

- ▸ The point of chapter 8 in *Win with People*, "Win with Your Team," is that ministry is a team sport. Jesus demonstrated this by investing deeply in His disciples, knowing that the mission He began would be carried forward by others.

- ▸ The goal of this session is to connect the three traits from chapter 7 that best reflect a shepherding approach—character, competency, and curiosity—with how those traits bless and build up a ministry team.

Follow-Up, Session 7

Circle back to the "Win This Week" challenge given at the end of session 7 by asking your team the questions below.

In session 7, you were given the challenge of focusing on one of the three Cs for seven days.

- Which "C"—character, competency, or curiosity—did you choose, and why?
- What observations did you have?

Talk About It

Since you may not have time to address everything in this section, note the questions that are most relevant to your team and start with those.

1. The questions in the following box appear at the end of chapter 8 in *Win with People*. Ask your team to share a few of their responses.

DISCUSSION

1. "Ministry is a team sport." Why is this important to remember?

2. After reading the chapter, how would you define the three characteristics of a good teammate?

   A. Character –
   B. Competency –
   C. Curiosity –

3. Which of the three characteristics of a good teammate is most important? Why?

APPLICATION

1. **Personal Reflection:** Think about the three characteristics of a good teammate. How well are you doing in these areas?

   A. Rate yourself for each of these characteristics on a scale of 1-10.

   B. Where are you doing well?

   C. Where do you need to grow?

2. **Action Step:** Set up a time to talk with your pastor or ministry leader this week.

    A. Share your assessment with them and ask for their honest feedback. Ask for areas where you can grow.

2. Read Ecclesiastes 4:9-10:

ECCLESIASTES 4:9-10

Two are better than one, because they have a good return for their labor: If either of them falls down, one can help the other up.

- How might this passage support the idea from the chapter that "ministry is a team sport"?

3. Copy the grid on a whiteboard, and then as a group write down specific characteristics or behaviors that reflect each trait. A few examples have been provided.

Demonstration of Character	Demonstration of Competency	Demonstration of Curiosity
Ex. Integrity	*Ex. Fruitful in work*	*Ex. Obvious desire to learn*
Ex. Undeniable love for Jesus	*Ex. Clear ability to lead effectively*	*Ex. Always asks good questions*

Once you have captured the team's thoughts, ask:

- As a team, how effectively are we hitting these marks?
- If we were to focus on just one of the three categories for the next six months, which should we choose, and why?
- When adding new staff members or volunteers to our existing team, which of the three do you think is most important for getting us where we want to go?
- Jesus invested in disciples who were imperfect but willing. How should we balance grace with high standards in all three categories both when selecting team members and in developing them once they join our team?

Win This Week

Give the following challenge to your team, and then close in prayer.

Share your team's 3 Cs assessment with a trusted ministry leader outside of your department and ask for honest feedback.

Ask how your team is perceived and what steps they would recommend taking to improve areas that seem to lag.

Come to the next meeting ready to share how this conversation challenged and encouraged you as a group.

SESSION 9

HOW TO HELP THE HERD WIN

We don't want graspers,
we want growers.

Win with People, p. 143

SESSION PREP

Before you meet with your team to work through this session:

- ☐ **Book** | Read chapter 9 in *Win with People*. Highlight anything that grabs your attention.
- ☐ **Leader Guide** | Skim the chapter 9 discussion questions and application steps on page 66. (They also appear in the book at the end of chapter 9.) Note the ones that are most relevant to your team right now.
- ☐ **Leader Guide** | Preview the "Talk About It" section so you can lead the discussion with thoughtful input.

SESSION GOAL

Keep these two things in mind:

- The point of chapter 9 in *Win with People*, "How to Help the Herd Win," is that because culture and behaviors are contagious, leaders must model and celebrate positive, faith-filled attitudes and address unhealthy team dynamics.
- The goal of this session is to help your team identify and develop "growers" in the church—people who are empowerment-minded, others-focused, servant-minded, and who "speak life."

Follow-Up, Session 8

Circle back to the "Win This Week" challenge given at the end of session 8 by asking your team the questions below.

In session 8, you were given the challenge of inviting a ministry leader to respond to your team's 3 Cs assessment.

- Whose insight did you seek, and why?
- What input did he or she provide, and what impact did it have?

Talk About It

Since you may not have time to address everything in this section, note the questions that are most relevant to your team and start with those.

1. The questions in the following box appear at the end of chapter 9 in *Win with People*. Ask your team to share a few of their responses.

DISCUSSION

1. How can fear and frustration lead to compromising values when developing teams? How can church leaders avoid this trap?

2. What is the difference between a shepherd and a hired hand?

3. Which of the differences between graspers and growers, listed on pages 144-146, is the most challenging for you personally? Explain.

APPLICATION

1. **Personal Reflection:** Consider your own ministry role:

   A. Are there areas where you have focused too much on position or personal gain rather than serving and shepherding others?

   B. What changes can you make to better embrace the qualities of a "grower" in your role?

2. **Action Step:** Based on your reflection above, identify one action you can take this week to adopt a "grower" mentality.

2. Read Philippians 2:3-4 aloud. Then, ask your team the questions that follow.

PHILIPPIANS 2:3-4

Do nothing out of selfish ambition or vain conceit. Rather, in humility value others above yourselves, not looking to your own interests but each of you to the interests of the others.

- In what situations do you sense the greatest tension between valuing others above yourself and getting things done efficiently in ministry? How can we balance humility and responsibility?

- How can we tell the difference between serving out of true humility and serving in a way that still centers on ourselves, (like wanting recognition or feeling indispensable)?

- What is one practical way that we as a team can make sure we're looking to the interests of others, both in how we serve our church and in how we work together?

3. The chapter describes five key differences between "graspers" and "growers."

Review the list noted below, and then have your team respond to the questions that follow:

Graspers start with position while growers start with heart.

Graspers pull things to themselves but growers know how to empower others.

Graspers think "me" but growers think "we."

Graspers are opportunists while growers are servants.

Graspers are critical but growers speak life.

- Which of these distinctions stand out most to you and why?

- Have you ever worked with a grasper? How did it affect the team or even the ministry at large?

- What are some ways that we can intentionally develop growers within our team?

Win This Week

Give the following challenge to your team, and then close in prayer.

Identify one person on our team who may need encouragement. Ask God to help you see their "grower" contributions; then, take time to seek him or her out and speak life over their work.

Come to the next meeting ready to share how things went.

SESSION 10

PROTECTING YOUR WINNING CULTURE

You instruct the simple, you challenge the fool, and you drive out the wicked.

Win with People, p. 165

SESSION PREP

Before you meet with your team to work through this session:

- ☐ **Book** | Read chapter 10 in *Win with People*. Highlight anything that grabs your attention.

- ☐ **Leader Guide** | Skim the chapter 10 discussion questions and application steps on page 74. (They also appear in the book at the end of chapter 10.) Note the ones that are most relevant to your team right now.

- ☐ **Leader Guide** | Preview the "Talk About It" section so you can lead the discussion with thoughtful input.

SESSION GOAL

Keep these two things in mind:

- ▸ The point of chapter 10 in *Win with People*, "Protecting Your Winning Culture," is understanding that culture is what shapes our teams, churches, and organizations. It is what we cultivate and defend.

- ▸ The goal of this session is to help your team see and seize two essential approaches to protecting the heart of your ministry: direct confrontation and cultural clarity.

Follow-Up, Session 9

Circle back to the "Win This Week" challenge given at the end of session 9 by asking your team the questions below.

In session 9, you were given the challenge of speaking life over another team member for one of their recent "grower" contributions.

- Who did you approach, and why?
- What did the encounter teach you?

Talk About It

Since you may not have time to address everything in this section, note the questions that are most relevant to your team and start with those.

1. The questions in the following box appear at the end of chapter 10 in *Win with People*. Ask your team to share a few of their responses.

DISCUSSION

1. Have you considered protecting the sheep as a core aspect of pastoral ministry? How does this affect your understanding of your role as a shepherd?

2. Give examples of situations where direct confrontation is necessary in pastoral ministry. How do these situations differ when addressing the simple, the fool, or the wicked?

3. How would you describe your church's "cultural clarity" regarding its mission, values, and processes? Is there a clear path for members to grow spiritually and serve?

APPLICATION

1. **Personal Reflection:** Reflect on the concept of a "tuning fork" for cultural clarity. What is your church's tuning fork, and how can you ensure it resonates consistently?

2. **Action Step:** Develop a plan to address the following:

    A. Identify one area of your ministry where cultural clarity could be strengthened. What can you do to more closely align that area with the mission of your church?

    B. Is there anyone in your church or ministry you've avoided confronting? What specific steps will you take to address it?

2. Because a healthy church is built on what it's for more than on what it's against, have your team spend a few minutes thinking through the values that guide you as a church. Write their input on a whiteboard.

3. Next, ask how your church's values show up in your team's everyday approach to ministry. How do you handle violations to these values now? After reading this chapter, are there any changes you'd make in how you handle these challenges?

Win This Week

Give the following challenge to your team, and then close in prayer.

Identify one potential cultural threat in your ministry area—whether a mindset, teaching, or relational dynamic. Take one proactive step this week to reinforce a healthy culture, whether through a conversation, a team meeting, or acting on one of your core values.

Come to the next meeting ready to share what you learned.

SESSION

11

THE MULTI-DIMENSIONAL SHEPHERD

If we take good care of the sheep,
they reproduce and multiply.
The same is true of our teams.
It's our responsibility to lead them well.

Win with People, p. 190

SESSION PREP

Before you meet with your team to work through this session:

- ☐ **Book** | Read chapter 11 in *Win with People.* Highlight anything that grabs your attention.

- ☐ **Leader Guide** | Skim the chapter 11 discussion questions and application steps on pages 80-81. (They also appear in the book at the end of chapter 11.) Note the ones that are most relevant to your team right now.

- ☐ **Leader Guide** | Preview the "Talk About It" section so you can lead the discussion with thoughtful input.

SESSION GOAL

Keep these two things in mind:

- The point of chapter 11 in *Win with People*, "The Multi-Dimensional Shepherd," is that a wise shepherd with a growing flock must possess expertise in terrain, weather, long-distance navigation, and resource identification. In ministry, this means he or she must care for the flock while preparing for expansion.

- The goal of this session is to prompt your team to excel as shepherds so that they naturally raise more shepherds.

Follow-Up, Session 10

Circle back to the "Win This Week" challenge given at the end of session 10 by asking your team the questions below.

In session 10, you were given the challenge of reinforcing a healthy culture by taking one proactive step.

- Which step did you take?
- What did you learn from the experience?

Talk About It

Since you may not have time to address everything in this section, note the questions that are most relevant to your team and start with those.

1. The questions in the following box appear at the end of chapter 11 in *Win with People*. Ask your team to share a few of their responses.

DISCUSSION

1. "Every opportunity to gain ground is not a God opportunity." Have you considered this thought before? Do you agree or disagree? Explain.

2. How can we balance the desire to expand our ministry with the responsibility of stewarding the people and the work God has already entrusted to us?

3. How can the concept of being a shepherd before becoming a rancher change how we pastor people?

APPLICATION

1. **Personal Reflection:** Honestly assess your motivation in ministry:

    A. Is your goal to be a rancher or a shepherd?

    B. Are you focused on getting bigger or getting better?

2. **Action Step:** Assess areas of your leadership or ministry where you need to "get better."

A. Identify two or three areas where you can improve.

B. Ask for feedback from your team and from trusted mentors.

C. Implement one specific change to grow in these areas this week.

2. Copy the grid onto a whiteboard. Then, talk with your team about the questions that follow.

STRATEGY ↑		
	Low Shepherding High Strategy **EFFICIENT ORGANIZER** Executor who often lacks relational warmth.	High Shepherding High Strategy **VISIONARY LEADER** Cares deeply while keeping big picture top of mind.
	Low Shepherding Low Strategy **DISCONNECTED DOER** Handles tasks reactively while also neglecting to engage relationally.	High Shepherding Low Strategy **HEARTFELT CAREGIVER** Loves people but lacks plan for long-term ministry effectiveness.
	SHEPHERDING →	

- Where would you place yourself on this grid? Is it where you want to stay? Why, or why not?

- Where would you place our team as a whole?

- Where would you rate me, as the leader of this team?

- Who from our team do you see as high/high? What do you see them regularly doing that leaves you with this impression?

3. Read 1 Corinthians 3:10, below, and then have your team engage with the following questions:

1 CORINTHIANS 3:10

By the grace God has given me, I laid a foundation as a wise builder, and someone else is building on it. But each one should build with care.

- What foundation are we laying for future ministry teams?

- How satisfied are we with that legacy?

- What changes do we need to make now to leave a legacy more in alignment with our God-given passion and gifting?

Win This Week

Give the following challenge to your team, and then close in prayer.

Before the next meeting, talk one-on-one with another member of your team. Allow time for both of you to answer this question:

- Based on this session's discussions, what would you say are two specific ways that my *getting better* would help our team's impact to *get bigger?*

Come to the next meeting prepared to share what you learned.

SESSION

12

WIN TODAY, WIN TOMORROW

Every time you love and serve God's people, you're hitting the bullseye.

—

Win with People, p. 206

SESSION PREP

Before you meet with your team to work through this session:

- ☐ **Book** | Read chapter 12 in *Win with People*. Highlight anything that grabs your attention.

- ☐ **Leader Guide** | Skim the chapter 12 discussion questions and application steps on page 88. (They also appear in the book at the end of chapter 12.) Note the ones that are most relevant to your team right now.

- ☐ **Leader Guide** | Preview the "Talk About It" section so you can lead the discussion with thoughtful input.

SESSION GOAL

Keep these two things in mind:

- The point of chapter 12 in *Win with People*, "Win Today, Win Tomorrow," is that as ministry leaders, we want to love, serve, and lead people well. Winning with people is not a one-time event; it's a lifelong commitment.

- The goal of this session is to prompt your team to assess five key areas: their personal relationship with Jesus, their clarity on their God-given calling, their quality of family life, their depth of relationship with the sheep, and the team's overall contribution to the mission of the church.

Follow-Up, Session 11

Circle back to the "Win This Week" challenge given at the end of session 11 by asking your team the questions below.

In session 11, you were given the challenge of asking another team member how your getting better would help the team's impact get bigger.

- Who did you choose to ask?
- What came of the conversation you had?

Talk About It

Since you may not have time to address everything in this section, note the questions that are most relevant to your team and start with those.

1. The questions in the following box appear at the end of chapter 12 in *Win with People*. Ask your team to share a few of their responses.

DISCUSSION

1. How does prioritizing your relationship with Jesus shape your leadership and calling?

2. How has your understanding of calling changed through this journey? What do you see differently now about your role in ministry?

3. What specific actions can you take to foster trust, communication, and clear vision within your team?

APPLICATION

1. **Personal Reflection:** Reflect on two important connections in your life:

    A. How is your relationship with Jesus? Are you allowing Him to shepherd you fully, or have you been operating on auto-pilot?

    B. How well are you prioritizing family right now? Are there any changes you need to make?

2. **Action Step:** Identify two or three people in your life to serve this week.

    A. Determine what you will do this week to help them feel what you feel. Consider the list on page 206 as a starting place.

2. As a team, engage with each of the five categories by answering the questions that follow.

Note: Reflection prompts have been provided after each category. Consider giving everyone time to write down their thoughts or prayers in their own journal.

Personal Relationship with Jesus

1. How would you assess the state of your personal relationship with Jesus? Are you leading on empty or being refreshed by Him daily?

2. What does it look like for you to "lie down in green pastures," as Psalm 23:2 calls it, in your current ministry season?

Reflection | What would it look like for me to lead from a place of refreshment?

Clarity of Calling

1. How has your understanding of your calling changed throughout this study?

2. Why is it essential to love the *process* of ministry, not just the output?

3. What are practical ways you can stay connected to your "why" in ministry?

Reflection | What practical changes can I make to stay connected to my "why" in ministry?

Quality of Family Life

1. Read aloud 1 Timothy 3:1-5 and Titus 1:6-9.

1 TIMOTHY 3:1-5

Here is a trustworthy saying: Whoever aspires to be an overseer desires a noble task. Now the overseer is to be above reproach, faithful to his wife, temperate, self-controlled, respectable, hospitable, able to teach, not given to drunkenness, not violent but gentle, not quarrelsome, not a lover of money. He must manage his own family well and see that his children obey him, and he must do so in a manner worthy of full respect. (If anyone does not know how to manage his own family, how can he take care of God's church?)

TITUS 1:6-9

An elder must be blameless, faithful to his wife, a man whose children believe and are not open to the charge of being wild and disobedient. Since an overseer manages God's household, he must be blameless—not overbearing, not quick-tempered, not given to drunkenness, not violent, not pursuing dishonest gain. Rather, he must be hospitable, one who loves what is good, who is self-controlled, upright, holy and disciplined. He must hold firmly to the trustworthy message as it has been taught, so that he can encourage others by sound doctrine and refute those who oppose it.

- What do these passages teach about leading our families well?

Reflection | Copy the following grid on a whiteboard and have each team member, in their own journal, evaluate how well they are investing in their family relationships. Have them consider some simple, accessible steps they might take to help close any gaps that exist.

Family Priority	Strength (1 to 10)	Next Step
Prayer Support		
Time Investment		
Spiritual Leadership		
Emotional Regulation		
Emotional Support		
Communication		
Other:		

Relationship with Sheep

1. Proverbs 27:23 says, "Be sure you know the condition of your flocks; give careful attention to your herds." How well do you know the spiritual condition of the people you lead?

2. What practical changes can you make to be more intentional about knowing and meeting the needs of the people you lead?

Reflection | Some things getting in my way of better knowing the people God has called me to lead are . . .

Team's Contribution

1. What's one thing our team does well in terms of vision, communication, and alignment?

2. What's one thing our team needs to improve to be more effective in shepherding people?

Reflection | A time when I felt proud of our team that I'd like to build on going forward was when . . .

Consider having a few team members share their response to the final reflection prompt before closing in prayer.